CRYPTO CURRENCY PROFIT FORMULA

Step By Step Guide To
Grow Your Wealth
With Crypto-currencies

Ashok Sharma

Copyright © 2017 Ashok Sharma

All rights reserved.

ISBN-10: 1976255295
ISBN-13: 978-1976255298

DEDICATION

This book is dedicated to
My mother who gave me
The best thing in life
life itself.

CONTENTS

1	What Is Cryptocurrency?	1
2	The Types Of Cryptocurrency Available	7
3	How To Open An Account To Invest	13
4	Strategies To Invest	27
5	How To Collect More Bitcoin	32
6	Why Buy Cryptocurrency?	37
7	Are There Any Drawbacks?	41
8	The Future Of Cryptocurrency	44

1. WHAT IS CRYPTOCURRENCY?

What is cryptocurrency? I'm sure many of you are curious of this so called "21st-century money of the future and due to its increasing recognition and security, the cryptocurrency market looks bright ahead.

By the end of this e-book, you'll certainly know more about cryptocurrency than most people out there. For this first chapter, we will be covering 5 topics :

1. What Is Cryptocurrency?
2. How DoCryptocurrencies Work?
3. How Are The Cryptocurrencies Value Determined?
4. What Is Cryptocurrency Used For?
5. Why Cryptocurrency?

What Is Cryptocurrency?

This is one of the most frequently asked questions out there. What is cryptocurrency? To make it simple, cryptocurrency is a digital version of money where the transactions are done online. A cryptocurrency is a medium of exchange just like your normal everyday currency such as the USD, but designed for the purpose of exchanging digital information through a process known as cryptography.

The first ever-successful cryptocurrency emerged from the invention of Bitcoin, by Satoshi Nakamoto. This was then followed by the birth of other types of crytocurrencies competing against Bitcoin.

How Do Cryptocurrencies Work?

Blockchains are built from 3 technologies		
1. Private Key Cryptography	2. P2P Network	3. Program (the blockchain's protocol)
Cash vs. Plastic	Tree falls in a forest	Tragedy of the commons
Identity	System of Record	Platform

The reason why cryptocurrenciesare such in demand right now is because Satoshi Nakamoto successfully found a way to build a decentralized digital cash system. What is a decentralized cash system?

A decentralized system means the network is powered by its users without having any third party, central authority or middleman controlling it. Not the central bank or the government has power over this system.

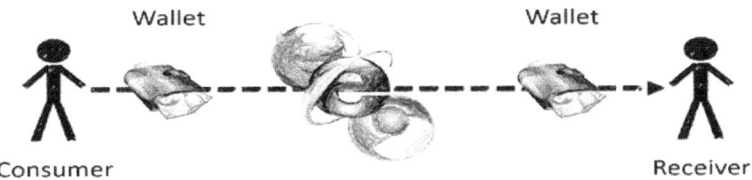

Decentralised

The problem with a centralized network in a payment system is the so called "double spending". Double spending happens when one entity spends the same amount twice. For instance, when you purchase things online, you have to incur for unnecessary and expensive transaction fees. Usually, this is done by a central server that keeps track of your balances.

What Are Miners Doing?
First and foremost, principally anyone can be miner. Miners are needed because of the nature of the decentralized network where they have no authority to delegate tasks and the cryptocurrency needs some kind of system to prevent any form of network abuse. For instance, a person may create thousands of peers and spread forged transactions. It will disrupt the system immediately.

In order for you to be a miner, you would need to solve a cryptologic puzzle which is a set of very complex mathematical questions set by Satoshi Nakamato himself. If you successfully solved the puzzle, as a miner you can build a block and add it to the blockchain.

The miner is also given permission to add a crypocurrency transaction to the system which automatically grants him a specific number of bitcoins. This is the only way to create valid bitcoins. Bitcoins can only be generated if a miner can solve a cryptographic puzzle. The level of difficulty increases with the amount of computer power the miners invest.

How Are The Cryptocurrencies Value Determined?

The value of cryptocurrencies are dependent on the market, where the prices of various cryptocurrencies vary a lot and is one of the most fluctuating and volatile markets to date.

The price of cryptocurrencies like any other products is dependent on demand and supply. If more people demands a particular currency and it is short in supply, then the value increases. More units are mined by miners to balance the flow. However, most currencies limit the supply of their tokens.

For instance the total amount of Bitcoin issued is only 21 million. Therefore Bitcoin's supply will decrease in time and will reach its final number by 2140. It also explains why Bitcoin's value is higher as compared to other cryptocurrencies.

Now you must be wondering, **what is cryptocurrency used for?**

Cryptocurrencies can be spent for different purposes and the best part is, all transactions are completed online! There are 3 different transactions that can be performed when using cryptocurrency:

1. **Bitcoin Trading**
2. **Personal Spending**
3. **Crowd Funding**

Firstly is **Bitcoin trading**.

Bitcoin trading can be very profitable for both professionals and beginners. The market is new, where arbitrage and margin trading is widely available. The currency's high volatility has also played a major role in bringing new investors to the trading market.

Compared to other financial currencies, Bitcoin has very little barrier to entry. If you already own Bitcoin, no verification is required and you can start trading almost instantly. Moreover, Bitcoin is not fiat currency. This simply means the price is not related to the economy or policies of any single country.

And unlike stock markets, there are no official Bitcoin exchanges. Instead, hundreds of Bitcoin exchanges operate 24/7 around the world. Because of no official exchanges, this results in no official Bitcoin price where the currency is known for its rapid and frequent price movements.

Secondly is **personal spending**. You can use Bitcoin to purchase almost anything! From buying cars to travelling the world.

In December 2013, a Tesla model S was purchased for a reported 91.4bitcoins. The dealer, located in California continues to accept Bitcoin as a means of payment. They have since managed to sell a Lamborghini Gallardo for 216.8 Bitcoin.

You can also travel the world using Bitcoins! Just head to www.cheapair.com. On 22nd November 2013, they announced that they would be the first online travelling agency accepting Bitcoin. You are able to purchase flights, hotels, car rentals and cruises. You can even book the whole package.

Cryptocurrency also provides the chance for you to **give back to society**. How? By crowd funding. You are able to be part of someone's success story by donating to a crypto crowd funding project. Companies such as Lighthouse have built their crowd funding platform using Bitcoin.

The perks of donating through this system are you will not be charged for your donation and funds will not be released unless the project meets its criteria. You are also able to withdraw from the campaign before its completion.

You have complete control over the donation! Examples of successful funding campaigns are from Dogecoin, which includes campaigns run for Nascar driver Josh Wise.

The question is, Why Cryptocurrency?

Apart from cryptocurrency being very secure and is run through a decentralized network, there are other properties which projects why cryptocurrencies may be the most talked about topic in town. It has also been considered as potentially an investment vehicle, which may garner massive returns.

Have you heard of Erik Finman? The teenage Bitcoin millionaire who started picking up Bitcoin at only $12 a piece back in May 2011, when he was just 12 years old. He received the Bitcoin as a tip from his brother and a $1000 gift from his grandmother.

He now reportedly owns 403 Bitcoins, which holds a value of roughly $2,600 where it has accumulated to a stash of $1.08 million and change.

There are various concrete reasons why you should invest in cryptocurrency. This will be elaborated further in chapter 6, but let me give you a brief summary on the perks of buying cryptocurrency.

Firstly are its transactional properties. Cryptocurrency transaction is fast and global. Transactions are propagated immediately in the network and are confirmed within minutes. Since the transactions are managed by a global network of computers, they do not take into account your physical location. It is possible for you to send your cryptocurrency to someone in your vicinity, or even if they are living on the other side of the world.

Secondly are their monetary properties. The currencies are in controlled supply thus there is a high chance that the value of the currencies appreciates over time. As mentioned earlier, Bitcoin will somehow reach its final number somewhere in 2140.

Third is their revolutionary property. You have more control of what is going on in your account and how the system works and operate. This is due to the decentralized network of peers which keeps a consensus on account balances and the transactions made. As compared to your physical bank account, which can be changed and controlled by people you don't see and governed by rules you don't even know?

2. THE TYPES OF CRYPTOCURRENCY AVAILABLE

The world of cryptocurrency has always revolved around Bitcoin until recently, when virtual currencies has served a very important purpose in the investment realm and people start flocking to cryptocurrencies as compared to fiat currencies.

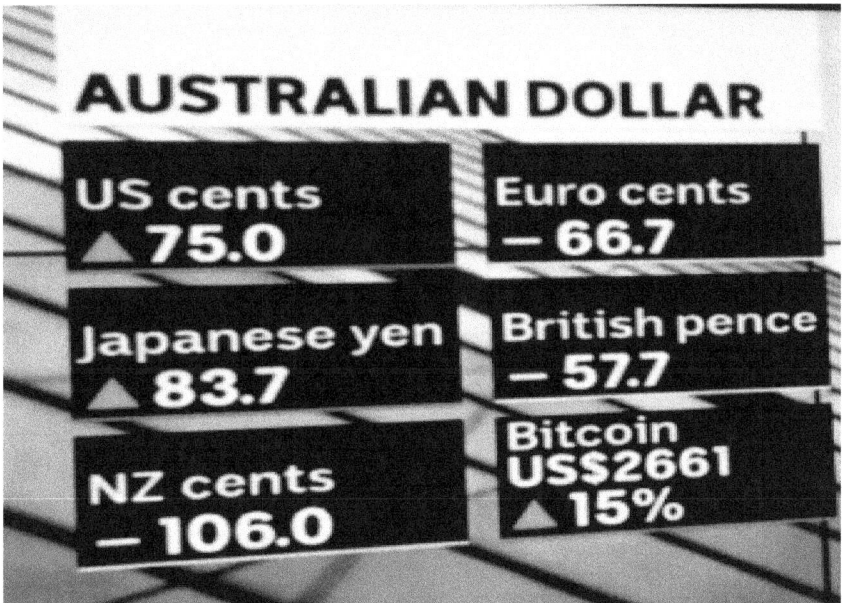

Believe it or not, aside from Bitcoin, there are over 800 cryptocurrencies! However, we will only discuss the top 5 most prominent currencies in the market. The 5 cryptocurrencies are:

1. Bitcoin
2. Ethereum
3. Litecoin
4. Monero
5. Ripple

Firstly, is **Bitcoin.**

This is the first ever cryptocurrency invented and remains by far the most sought after cryptocurrency to date. Bitcoin is known as the digital gold standard in the cryptocurrency network. As explained in the previous module, Bitcoin is the pioneer of Blockchain Technology that made digital money possible.

It is the first ever decentralized peer-to-peer network powered by its users without any central authority or middleman which means, no unnecessary costs are included in the digital money transaction.

Over the years of Bitcoin's existence, its value has fluctuated tremendously from zero to over $2000 per bitcoin to date. Its transaction volume has also reached 200,000 daily transactions.

One major advantage that it has over other crypotcurrencies is bitcoins are impossible to counterfeit or inflate. The reason being there are only 21 million bitcoins created for mining, no more no less. Therefore it is predicted by 2140, all bitcoins will already be mined.

Thanks to its blockchain technology, you have ultimate control over your money and transactions without having to go through a third party such as the bank or Paypal.

Bitcoin transactions are also impossible to be reversed. Therefore, you should only deal with trusted parties as Bitcoin is also used as a means for cyber-crime like dark net markets or ransomware.

Media companies and investment firms in South Korea, India, Australia and Japan have started discussing on how Bitcoin may surpass the value of certain fiat currencies in the future as an alternative monetary system.

ABC News, a national news service in Australia have also reported recently it is likely for Bitcoin to replace even the USD in the next 10 years if it sustains its current exponential growth.

The second most popular currency is **Ethereum**.

Created by Vitalik Buterin, it has scored itself the second spot in the hierarchy of cryptocurrencies. This digital currency launched in 2015 is predicted to surpass Bitcoin and may be the cryptocurrency of the future. Ethereum is currently worth $279 since its launch.

Is Ethereum similar to Bitcoin?

It is in a way, but not really. Like Bitcoin, Ethereum is a part of a blockchain network. The main difference between the two currencies is that Bitcoin blockchain focuses on tracking ownership of the digital currency while Ethereum blockchain focuses on running the programming code or network.

Instead of having to build an entirely original blockchain for each new application, Ethereum enables the development of thousands of different applications in a single platform. In the Ethereum blockchain, miners work to earn Ether. Ether is a crypto token that helps run the network.

Another use of the Ethereum blockchain is its ability to decentralize any services that are centralized. For instance, Ethereum is able to decentralize services like loans provided by banks, online transactions using Paypal as well as voting systems and much more.

Ethereum can also be used to build a Decentralized Autonomous Organization (DAO). A DAO is a fully autonomous organization without a leader. DAOs are run by programming codes on a collection of smart contracts written in the Ethereum blockchain. DAO is designed to replace the structure of a traditional organization and like Bitcoin, eliminating the need for people and a centralized control.

What are the most obvious benefits of Ethereum?

Firstly, a third party cannot make any changes to the data. The system is also tamper and corruption proof. This is because Ethereum is built based on a network formed around a consensus as a result, making censorship impossible.

Secondly, just like Bitcoin, Ethereum is backed up by secure cryptography. Therefore, the applications are well protected against any form of hacking.

The third cryptocurrency is **Litecoin**.

When the currency was first launched in 2011, it aspired to be the 'silver' to Bitcoin's 'gold'. Litecoin also recorded the highest market cap of any other mined cryptocurrency, after Bitcoin after its launch.

The main reason of Litecoin's creation is to make up what Bitcoin lacked. The main difference between Litecoin and Bitcoin is the 2.5 minute time to generate a block for Litecoin, as opposed to Bitcoin's 10 minutes.

For miners and technical experts, the Litecoin possesses a very important difference to Bitcoin, and that is a more improved work algorithm which speeds up the hashing power and system altogether.

One of the biggest advantages that Litecoin possesses is it can handle a higher volume of transactions thanks to its algorithm. The faster block time also prevents double spending attacks.

While Litecoin failed to secure and maintain its second place after Bitcoin, it is still actively mined and traded and is bought by investors as a backup in case Bitcoin fails. The current value of Litecoin is $46.

The fourth currency is **Monero**.

This digital currency was launched in 2014 and it's main goal was to create an algorithm to add the privacy features that is missing in Bitcoin. Monero invented a system known as the "ring signatures" to conceal the identity of its senders and recipients.

Ring signatures combine a user's private account keys with public keys obtained from Monero's blockchain to create a ring of possible signers that would not allow outsiders to link a signature to a specific user.

While Monero users have the ability to keep their transactions private, they are also able to share their information selectively. Every Monero account has a "view key", which allows anyone holding it to view the account's transactions.

Initially, the ring signature system concealed the senders and recipients involved in the Monero transactions without hiding the amount being transferred. However, an updated and improved version of the ring signature system known as "Ring CT" enabled the value of individual transactions as well as its recipients to be hidden.

Apart from ring signatures, Monero also improved its privacy settings by using "Stealth Addresses", which are randomly generated, one time addresses. These addresses are created for each transaction on behalf of the recipients.

With this feature, the recipients use a single address and transactions they receive go to separate, unique addresses. This way, Monero transactions cannot be linked to the published address of the recipients.

By providing a high level of privacy, Monero allows each unit of its individual currency to be exchanged between one another. Meaning, each of its coin has the same value.

Like the other cryptocurrencies, Monero offers interested parties to mine blocks. Individuals may choose to join a mining pool, or they may mine Monero by themselves.

Anyone with a computer can mine Monero, as they do not require any specific hardware or specific integrated circuits like Bitcoin. Instead, Monero utilizes a Proof-of-Work (PoW) Algorithm that is designed to accept a wide range of processors, a feature which was included to ensure that mining was open to all parties.

The price of Monero has fluctuated quite frequently from its launch until May 2017, where the current value of the currency is now $43.80.

Monero has received the acceptance of multiple dark web marketplaces and has generated its own fan base due to its privacy settings. Therefore, it is less speculative as compared to other digital currencies and traders purchase Monero as a hedge for other cryptocurrencies.

Last but not least is **Ripple**.

Ripple is actually a technology that has a dual function; as a digital currency as well as a digital payment network for financial transactions. It was launched in 2012 and co-founded by Chris Larsen and Jed McCaleb. The cryptocurrency coin under Ripple is labeled as XRP.

Unlike the other cryptocurrencies, Ripple operates on an open-source and a peer-to-peer decentralized platform which allows a transfer of money in any form, both fiat and cryptocurrency

Ripple uses a middleman in the currency transactions. The medium (the middleman) known as "Getaway" acts as a link in the network between two parties wanting to make a transaction.

The way it works is that the Gateway functions as a credit intermediary that receives and sends currencies to public addresses over the Ripple network. This is why Ripple is less popular when compared to the other digital currencies, with only a $0.26 value to date.

Ripple's digital coin, XRP acts as a bridge for other currencies which includes both fiat and cryptocurrencies. In Ripple's network, any currency can be exchanged between one another.

If user X wants Bitcoins as the form of payment for his services from Y, then Y does not necessarily have to possess Bitcoins. Y can pay X to X's Gateway using US Dollars or any other currencies. X will then receive Bitcoins converted from the US Dollars from his Gateway.

The nature of Ripple's network and its systems exposes its users to certain risks. Even though you are able to exchange any currencies, the Ripple network does not run with a proof-of-work system like Bitcoin. Instead, transactions are heavily reliant on a consensus protocol in order to validate account balances and transactions on the system.

But Ripple does improve some features of traditional banks. Namely, transactions are completed within seconds on a Ripple network even though the system handles millions of transactions frequently.

Unlike traditional banks, even a wire transfer may take up days or weeks to complete. The fee to conduct transactions on Ripple is also very minimal, as opposed to large fees charged by banks to complete cross-border payments.

3. HOW TO OPEN AN ACCOUNT TO INVEST

To start investing in cryptocurrencies, the first thing you would need is to set up your digital wallet. In the cryptocurrency realm, the term used is "wallet". The wallet can be likened to a bank account, which can be stored in different devices.

A cryptocurrency wallet is a software program that functions to store private and public keys and interacts with various blockchains. It enables users to send and receive cryptocurrencies as well as tracking their balance.

There are many wallets out there for you to choose from, which is all dependent on your security needs as well as whether you wish to be an active trader or a more passive buy-and-hold investor.

Once you have set up your wallet, you can then proceed to purchase and exchange the digital currency of your choice on many platforms. Firstly, let's explore the top 5 wallets for you to choose from to hold your crypto funds.

The top 5 wallets that you can choose from to store your cryptocurrencies are as follows:

1. breadwallet.com
2. Blockchain.info
3. Coinpayment
4. Coinbase
5. Unocoin (Indian Bitcoin Wallet).

Firstly, let's look at **breadwallet.com**.

For now, breadwallet only receives Bitcoin to store in their digital wallets. This wallet is great for Bitcoin beginners as it is very user friendly and simple to use. Most importantly, the tool is free to use.

All you need to do is to download breadwallet, choose a passcode and you are ready to receive your currencies. There are no login names or passwords and no complicated cryptographic keys or configuring any settings.

However, the downside of this wallet is that it can only be downloaded to your mobile device and there is no web or desktop interfaces. It also lacks features and it is a hot wallet, which means it has less security and other parties may access your private keys easier.

The second wallet is known as **Blockchain.info**.

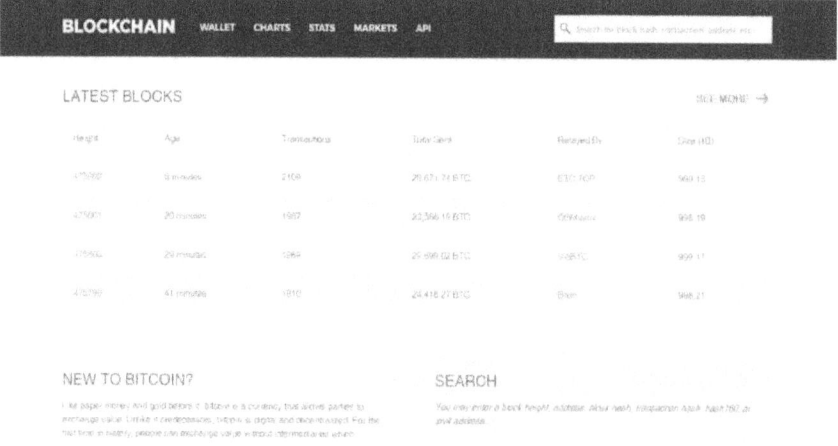

The Blockchain is catered towards Bitcoins only and is a mobile based app for both iOS and Android. It also acts as a web based wallet. The most distinguishable feature of the Blockchain wallet is the newly developed payment channel for the Bitcoin network, known as "Thunder".

The technology enables users to send and receive Bitcoins without touching the main blockchain. This results in a very secure transaction and instant payments.

The Blockchain wallet is free and to create your account, you need to head to the main page and sign up for your account.

The third wallet is known as **Coinpayment.**

Over 378,500 vendors across 182 different countries. Coin payments is the first and largest payment processor of over 75 crypto currencies.

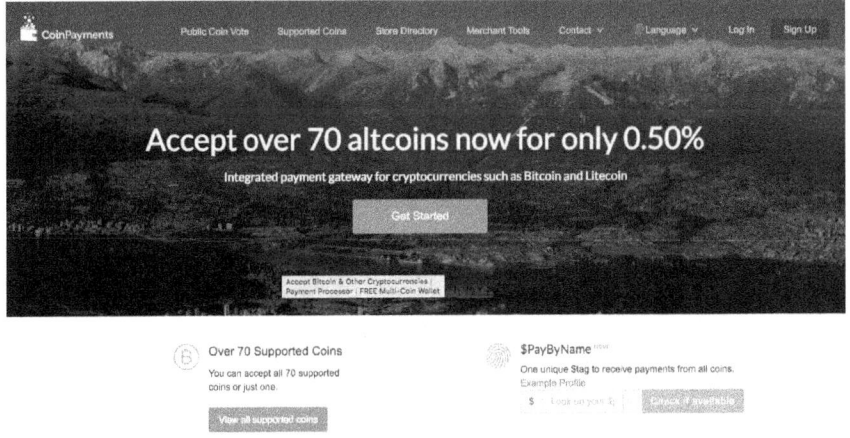

Next is **Coinbase**.

With Coinbase you can send bitcoin to ashok sharma or anyone else in the world. Because ashok sharma referred you, when you sign up and buy or sell $100 of bitcoin or more, you'll both earn $10 of free bitcoin!

Last but not least is **Unocoin (Indian Bitcoin Wallet)**.

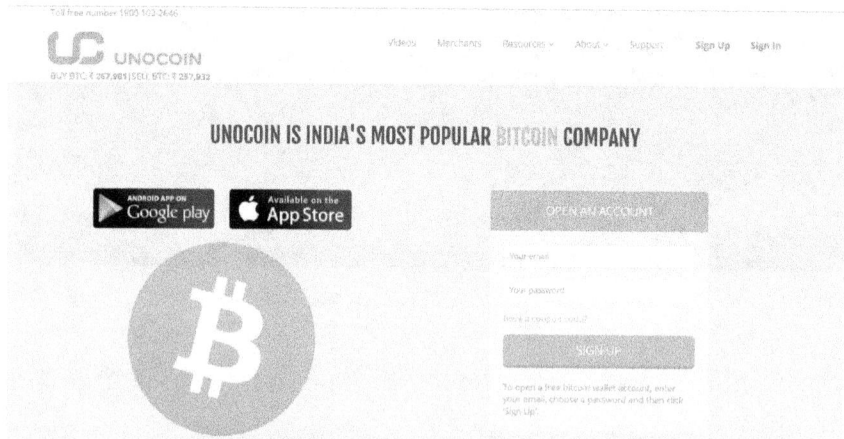

UNOCOIN IS INDIA'S MOST POPULAR BITCOIN COMPANY. Start buying and selling bitcoin through your Indian bank account. Store your bitcoin securely in your Unocoin wallet or vault. Accept bitcoin from your friends and customers around the world.

We've already discussed the platforms where you can hold your cryptocurrencies. As mentioned previously, the wallets can be stored in different devices.

There are 5 types of devices where you can download and store your wallets to hold your cryptocurrencies:

1. **Desktop**
2. **Cloud**
3. **Mobile Devices**
4. **Hardware**
5. **Paper**

Firstly, is your **desktop**.

Your wallets can be downloaded on a PC or laptop. They are only accessible from the single computer in which they are downloaded. It offers very good security but the drawback is you are only able to access your wallet on the desktop and nowhere else.

The second drawback is when your PC is attacked by virus, the virus may also affect your cryptocurrency wallet and your wallet may get hacked. The virus may also access your private keys and your funds.

Secondly, your wallet can be downloaded and stored in **cloud or online**. The wallets run on the cloud and are accessible from any devices in any location.

They are very convenient to access unlike your wallets stored on the desktop. However, bear in mind that your private keys are stored online and other parties may potentially access your wallet easily.

The next wallet is your **mobile wallet.** You can download your wallet on your mobile device via the App Store or Google Playstore and others. Having your wallet on your mobile makes it very convenient as you have access to it anywhere you go.

A lot of them are quite secure as they have multiple signature accesses as well as backup features in case you lose your phone. This way you would not risk losing your crypto funds as the backup feature has backed up your private key to unlock your wallet.

The fourth wallet is your **hardware wallet**. A hardware wallet means you store your crypto funds on a USB or hard drive. Although hardware wallets complete their transactions online, they are stored offline and this enhances the security.

Last but not least is you can store your wallet on **paper**. Paper wallets are wallets printed out on a piece of paper. They are very easy to use as you have the option to carry it wherever you go, or you can even store it somewhere safe.

Because they are printed out, they provide a very high level of security. While the term paper wallet can refer to a physical copy or printout of your public and private keys, it can also refer to a piece of software used to securely generate a pair of keys which are then printed.

Now this leaves us with an important question, where should you store your wallet which contains your crypto funds?

This all depends on whether you are an active or passive user of cryptocurrency. To asses which user you are, you need to answer the following questions:

1. Do you need a wallet for everyday purchases, or just buying and holding your digital currency?

2. Do you plan to use several currencies or just one single currency?

3. Do you require access to your digital wallet wherever you are, even when you are on the go or only from home?

For instance, if you are the type of user who constantly spends your crypto funds to purchase daily necessities, you may want to store your wallet in your mobile device or on cloud.

However, if you plan to buy and hold your currencies for future investments, it is best for you to store your wallet on a hardware or paper wallet.

Once you have chosen the best platform to hold your currencies, you can now proceed to the many digital currency exchanges to purchase your cryptocurrency and kick start your investment!

Cryptocurrency Exchanges For Investment

First and foremost, let's get familiar with cryptocurrency exchanges. What is cryptocurrency exchange? Cryptocurrency exchanges are websites which allows you to buy, sell and exchange cryptocurrencies for other digital currency or fiat currencies like USD or Euro.

If you are very well versed in your crypto investment game and are used to trade professionally, you will likely need to use an exchange platform that requires you to open an account and verify your identification.

However if you are relatively new to the realm of cryptocurrency as a beginner I advise to start with platforms which do not require you to open an account. These exchanges are usually very straightforward and you can start trading occasionally until you get the hang of it.

There are 3 types of cryptocurrency exchanges:

1. **Trading Platforms**

    These are websites that connects buyers and sellers where they charge certain fees for a completed transaction.

2. **Direct Trading**

    These platforms offer direct person to person exchange. You may exchange with individuals from different countries as well as different currencies. Direct trading does not necessarily adhere to the market price, as the individuals trading may set their own exchange rate.

3. **Brokers**

    These are websites that anyone can visit to purchase cryptocurrencies. However, the price is set by the broker. Cryptocurrency brokers are similar to foreign exchange dealers.

Before making your first trade, it's important to take note of these 5 key information to minimize your risk and maximize your return on investment.

1. **Reputation**
    Before you start your exchange on your selected site, ensure you've gathered sufficient information regarding the site such as reviews from professional traders as well as well-known industry websites. You may also join forums that discussescryptocurrency issues such as Bitcoin Talk or Reddit.

2. **Fees**

    Most exchanges will have fee-related information on their websites. Before joining any sites, ensure you have understood the exchange jargons; deposit, transaction and withdrawal fees. Fees may vary according to the exchange you choose.

3. **Payment Methods**

    Take note of the payment method available. Does the site use credit and debit card? Wire transfer? PayPal? If a particular exchange has very limited payment methods then it may not be convenient for you. Always remember that purchasing currencies via credit card will always require an ID verification and it comes with a premium price to increase the security measures.

    Meanwhile, purchasing cryptocurrency via wire transfer will take longer as it takes time for banks to process.

4. **Verification Requirements**

    Majority of Bitcoin's trading platforms both in the US and the UK require a form of ID verification to make deposits and withdrawals. Some exchanges will also allow you to remain anonymous. Bear in mind that verifications may take up days but this is protect exchanges from any sort of money laundering.

5. **Exchange Rate**

    Do not be surprised that different exchanges offer different rates. Therefore, always remember to shop around and to not immediately settle on an exchange. This makes a big difference on your investment as cryptocurrencies are known to fluctuate in value up to 10% and even higher in some circumstances.

As cryptocurrency is gaining more attention around the globe, there is a vast array of exchange platforms to choose from. But not all exchange platforms are created equal. These are the top 7 most visited exchange platforms in no particular order.

1. **Coinbase**
2. **Kraken**
3. **Cex.io**
4. **ShapeShift**
5. **Poloniex**
6. **Bittrex**
7. **novaexchange**

Firstly, is **Coinbase**.

Coinbase is one of the most popular exchange platforms to date. It is used by trusted investors and millions of investors around the globe. This platform is user friendly as it makes it easy for you to securely buy, use, store and trade digital currency.

The platform allows you to exchange currencies like Bitcoin, Ethereum, and recently, Litecoin. They also have a digital wallet that is available on iPhone and Android.

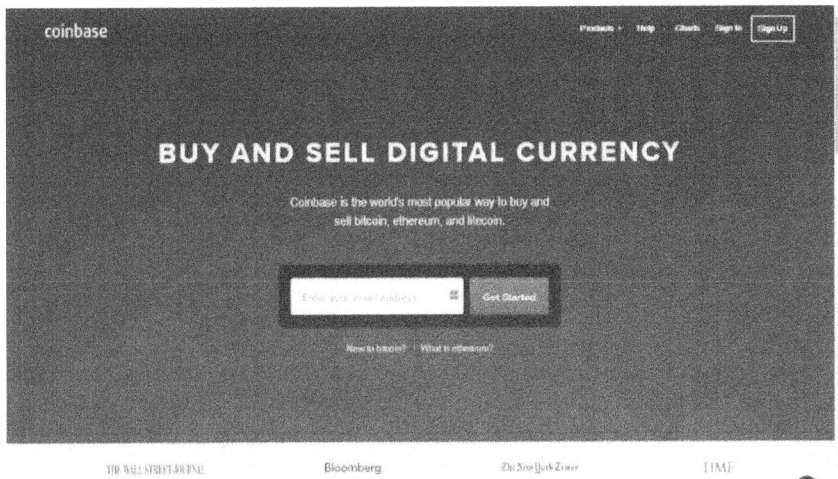

However, the selection of tradable currencies are dependent on the country you live in. Currently, Coinbase only allows transactions in the US, Europe, UK,

Canada, Australia and Singapore. The method of payment is also quite limited and restricted to bank transfers, credit/debit cards and PayPal. To get started, all you need to do is to sign up for your account and you are good to go!

The second platform is **Kraken**.

Kraken is the largest Bitcoin exchange in euro volume and liquidity and is the first partner in the cryptocurrency bank. Kraken allows the exchange of Bitcoins, where you are also able to trade Bitcoins and euros, US Dollars, Canadian Dollars, British Pounds and Japanese Yen.

Kraken also allows the trade of other digital currencies such as Ethereum, Monero, Ethereum Classic, Augur REP tokens, Litecoin, ICONOMI, Zcash and many more.

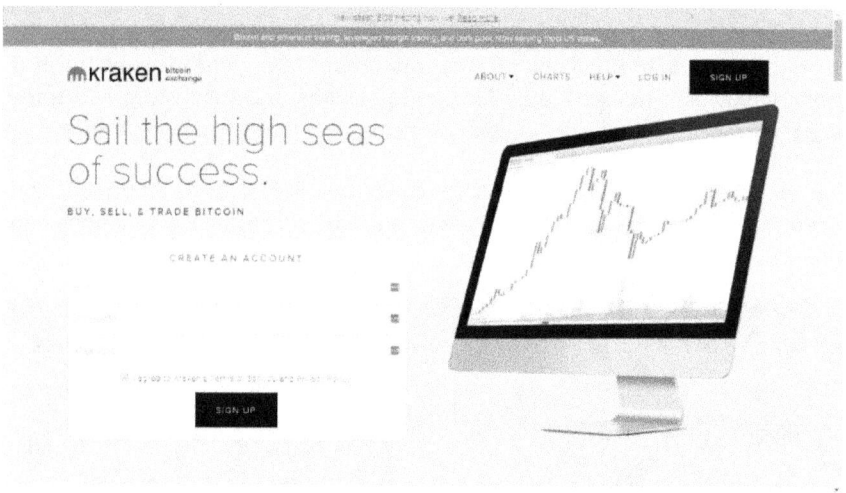

Kraken also caters towards more experienced users where it offers margin trading and other advanced trading features. Cost wise, Kraken has very decent exchange rates, low transaction fees as well as minimal deposit fees.

However, like Coinbase, the payment methods are also very limited. Kraken is also more suitable for advanced traders and investors and it may be a little difficult for newcomers as it has an unintuitive user interface.

To open up a basic account to start trading, you need to sign up for your account on their main page where it requires your personally details. A more advanced account additionally requires a government issued ID and a proof of residence.

The third exchange platform is **Cex.io**.

This platform enables its users to easily trade fiat currency with cryptocurrencies and vice versa. For traders looking to trade Bitcoins professionally, the platform offers personalized and user-friendly trading dashboards and margin trading.

CEX also offers a brokerage service which provides inexperienced traders a very simple way to purchase Bitcoins according to the market rate. CEX is a very practical mobile product where it is supported worldwide and has a very decent exchange rate. However, depositing currencies in your account is quite expensive.

To start your trading on CEX, you need to head on to the mainpage and sign up for your account.

Next up is **ShapeShift**.

ShapeShift is tailored towards users who wish to make instant straightforward trades without signing up for an account or relying on a platform to hold your funds.

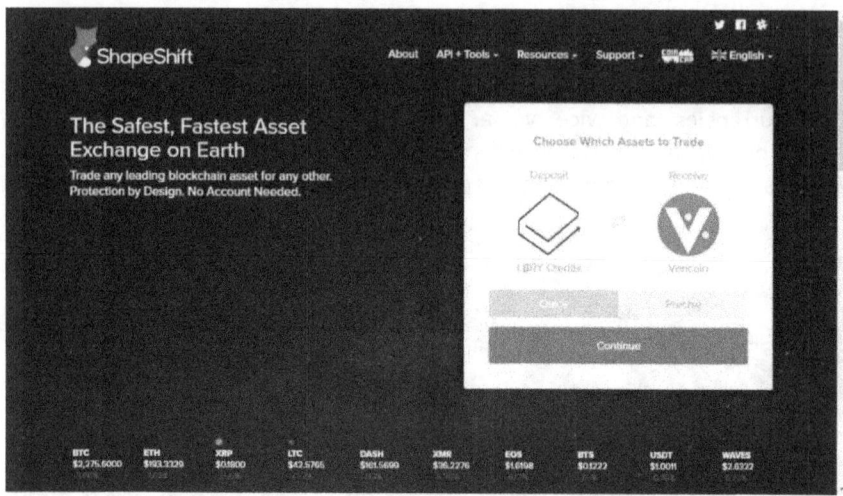

It also supports the exchange of multiple cryptocurrencies including Bitcoin, Ethereum, Monero, Zcash and many more. However, it does not allow fiat currency exchange with cryptocurrencies and the payment methods are very limited as users are not allowed to purchase their digital currencies with debit/credit cards or any other payment system. Payments are to be done via cryptocurrencies only.

Last but not least is **Poloniex**.

This platform offers a secure trading environment with more than 100 different Bitcoincryptocurrency pairings and advanced features for professional investors.

Poloniex has a fee schedule for all its traders. Therefore, the fee that is charged varies depending on if you are a maker or a taker. Makers are traders who displays their orders on the order prior to the trade. Takers are users who "takes" the makers order.

For makers, their fees range from 0 to 0.15% depending on the amount traded. For takers, fees range from 0.10 to 0.25%. The reason why the fees vary is because maker-taker model encourages market liquidity by rewarding the makers of that liquidity with a fee discount.

CRYPTO CURRENCY PROFIT FORMULA

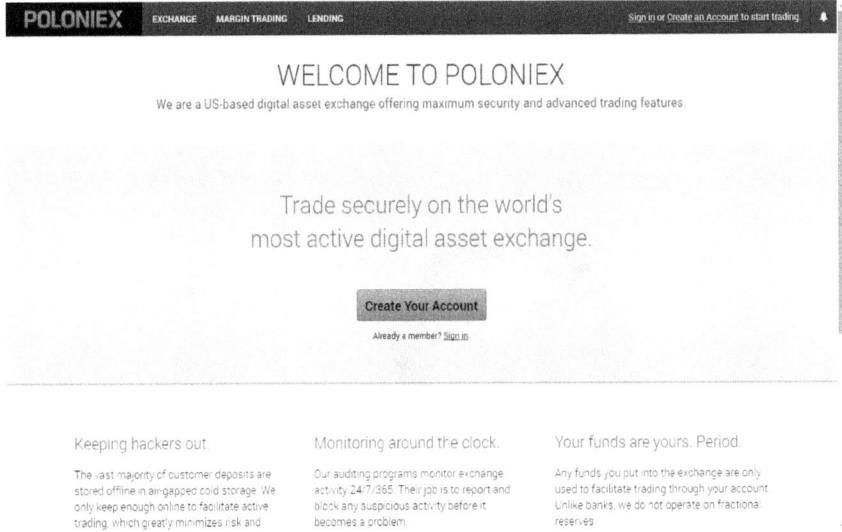

In order to start trading, you have to sign up for an account on Poloniex's mainpage.

To start investing, you have to firstly possess a digital wallet. Then, shop around for suitable exchange platforms according to your preferences. The main factor to take into account before starting your investment is to acknowledge whether you are an active or passive user of cryptocurrency; are you in it for the short-term, or the long-run?

Similarly you can exchange with

- **Bittrex.com**

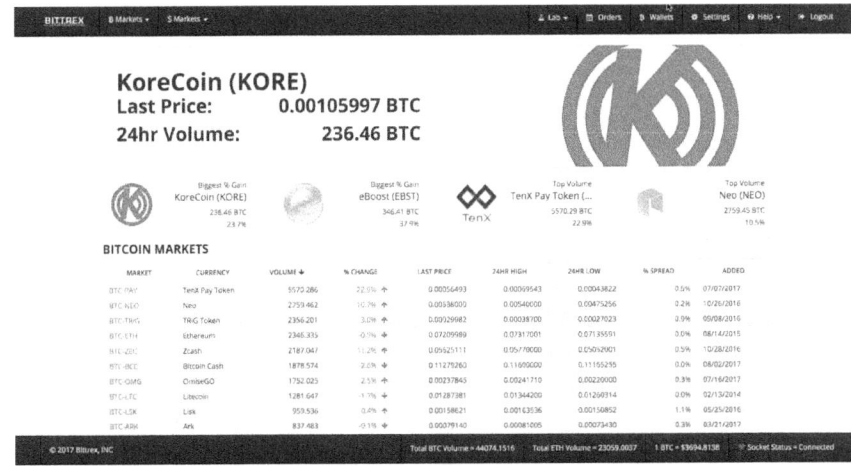

- **Novaexchange.com**

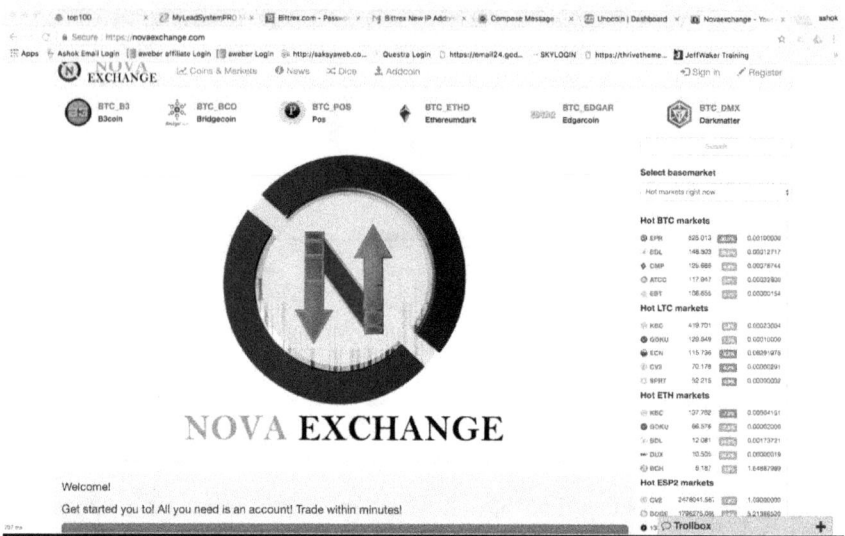

4. STRATEGIES TO INVEST

Investing in cryptocurrencies comes with its own risks as well as rewards. Therefore, you need to invest strategically in order to maximize your return on investment and minimize your risks. There are specific strategies you need to adopt to ensure a successful cryptocurrency investment and building your portfolio.

There are 5 strategies, which may come in handy for you especially if you are relatively new to the cryptocurrency realm.

1. Understand the whole concept of cryptocurrency
2. Spy on the market
3. Invest in more than one coin
4. Start small and scale higher
5. Reallocate your investment

Firstly, it is important for you to understand the whole concept of cryptocurrency.

Always keep in mind that you do not simply invest in something you are not sure and uncertain of. Do not jump on the bandwagon and follow what other people are doing just because you fear of missing out. For instance, a lot of people see their peers investing in property and they just follow suit in hopes to generate millions without even conducting prior research.

Therefore the first thing you ought to do is to study the space. These are the important points to be digested before kick-starting your investment:

- **What is cryptocurrency?**
- **What is Blockchain Technology?**
- **What is Bitcoin?**
- **What are the other popular digital currencies?**
- **What are the coins market caps?**
- **How can you start your own cryptocurrency exchanges?**
- **Where can you make cryptocurrency exchanges?**

Take your time to understand the realm of cryptocurrency and don't rush the process. It may take weeks or even months to digest all the information but this step is imperative for you so you can be on top of the game and an expert in the field. This way, there's a very low chance for you to waste your resources as you are familiar with the cryptocurrency industry.

The second strategy to invest is to spy on the market.

What does spying on the market mean? Spying on the market means you are observing what is currently working in the crytocurrency market. What you want to specifically look into is:

- **What is the most sought after currency?**
- **What is the value of the currency?**
- **Which currency has the highest market cap?**
- **Should you buy and hold the currency for future investments?**

Always remember that the cryptocurrency market is very volatile and the values fluctuate every now and then. The values usually depend on a lot of factors such as the speculators, the market demand, the supply demand and different institutions manipulating the prices.

My advice is for you to shop around and do not settle immediately for a specific cryptocurrency just because it has the highest value or popularity at the moment.

For instance, the most sought after currency at the moment is Bitcoin, but many professional traders and investors have predicted that Ethereum may surpass Bitcoin and become the currency of the future in the coming years. Therefore, always spy on the market and analyze the information.

The next strategy is to invest in more than one cryptocurrency.

It is not wise to invest all of your money into a single digital currency. A well balanced portfolio minimizes your risk as when you possibly lose on a cryptocurrency you own, you can still gain with the other ones you have.

If you decide to invest in only one currency for example Litecoin, what if the whole currency collapses? You'll lose all of the money you have invested in a split second without any backups.

Therefore, always invest in 2 or more currencies. Constantly spy on the market and choose the currency you prefer.

The fourth strategy is to start small and scale higher as you go.

A lot of people assume you become instantly rich when you invest in cryptocurrency. However, that is not always the case. You don't just become rich once you choose to invest in cryptocurrency. There's a strategy and a learning curve to get where you want to be.

Therefore always remember to start small, especially for those who have a small risk appetite. As mentioned in the previous chapters, cryptocurrency values are very volatile in nature as it depends on many factors. The values fluctuate even more in this cryptocurrency season where many people are starting to trade digital currencies.

For beginners, the rule of thumb is to start investing $500 for your cryptocurrencies. You don't necessarily have to start investing thousands! Now that you have your $500, how do you divide the money and what currency do you start to purchase first?

Firstly, remember to sign up for your digital wallet, and deposit your fiat currency and purchase the top 2 cryptocurrencies; Bitcoin and Ethereum.

The reason why we're selecting the 2 is because they are the safest and established choice as compared to the other currencies. They are prone to fluctuation, but not as much for now.

So, you split the $500, and purchase $250 worth of Bitcoin and $250 for Ethereum. This is a smart way to do it and if there are chances of you losing any of your funds, the risk is still worth taking.

When you get the hang of it, you can scale your investment higher by purchasing your cryptocurrencies in a higher value.

Last but not least is to reallocate your investment.

Once you've completed all the steps from 1-4, which means you're familiar with the cryptocurrency realm, you can reallocate your funds according to the digital currency market.

When you've started trading and investing, you'll notice over a period of time some currencies will do better than others.

For instance, you've observed Bitcoin's market and it has gone up whereas Ethereum has gone down, you can drag your funds to the higher currency market. This means, you can play around according to what's working in the current market and constantly reallocate your money.

When you get the hang of it, you'll realize that your investment will build up eventually from $500 to $1000, from $1000 to possibly $100,000! Always remember to do your part in getting to know more of the cryptocurrency market as there is always something new to look into. Be strategic in your investment and only investment in what you know!

5. HOW TO COLLECT MORE BITCOIN

There are 6 methods for you to earn more Bitcoins and it is not only restricted to cryptocurrency exchange or trading. The 6 methods are:

1. **Cryptocurrency exchange**

2. **Faucets**

3. **Micro tasking**

4. **Supplying Bitcoin related services**

5. **Becoming a Bitcoin Escrow Agent**

6. **Bitcoin Affiliate Marketing**

The first method to collect more Bitcoins is by cryptocurrency exchange or trading.

As mentioned in the previous modules, there are various forms of trading or exchange options available for Bitcoin. You may trade Bitcoin for Bitcoin, or Bitcoin with other cryptocurrencies, and even Bitcoin with fiat currencies.

But most importantly, ensure you have equipped yourself with the knowledge required to start exchanging Bitcoin so you know the risks involved as well as how much you need to invest as a beginner.

One of the most common ways of accumulating and earning Bitcoin through trading is by "Day Trading". Day trading is the buying and selling of Bitcoins on the same day, based on small, short-term price fluctuations.

Therefore, when you observe the market and notice that the value of Bitcoin is going up, it's a good time to purchase some Bitcoins and sell them right away after you've made your profit.

The second method to earn Bitcoins is through "Faucets".

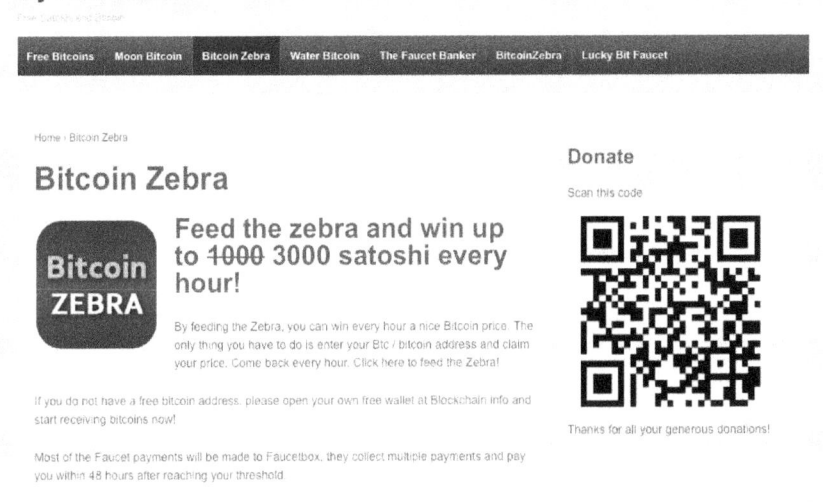

What are Faucets?

Faucets are websites which give away Bitcoins on a regular basis. They may give away Bitcoins every minute, every 10 minutes, every hour or once a week.

All you need to do is to sign up on the websites using your Bitcoin address and sometimes your email. And if you are selected, you get the Bitcoins.

However one downside to this method is the amount of Bitcoin given away is not as much, and sometimes the most you'll get is 0.00288BTC which equals to $1.31. But still, who would want to give you Bitcoins for free? And looking at how volatile the cryptocurrency market is, it is definitely worth the try!

Some of the popular Faucets that you can try to sign up to win your Bitcoins are:

- **Bitcoin Zebra**
- **Moon Bitcoin**
- **Weekend Bitcoin**
- **Milli**

The third method to earn your Bitcoin is by micro tasking.

Micro tasking is websites that pay their users using Bitcoins for completing tasks such as filling up surveys, watching videos and signing up for new services. You can sign up for free and all the tasks can be done within your own time! One example of a micro tasking site is Coinworker.

Next, you can earn Bitcoin by offering Bitcoin related services.

Not many people know that you can get paid with Bitcoin instead of Fiat Currency for offering Bitcoin related services. If you want to get an idea of what services you could offer you can visit Coinality, a site which gives current updates on Bitcoin jobs posted online.

You can also visit BitcoinTalk, a forum which discusses a wide range of cryptocurrency topics, including a services thread where users are searching for Bitcoin service providers.

Some examples of services people are looking for are:

- **Blockchain developer**
- **Website manager**
- **Graphic designer**
- **Mining expert**
- **Online marketer**
- **Writing for cryptocurrency blogs and news sites**

The fifth method for you to earn more Bitcoin is by becoming a Bitcoin Escrow agent.

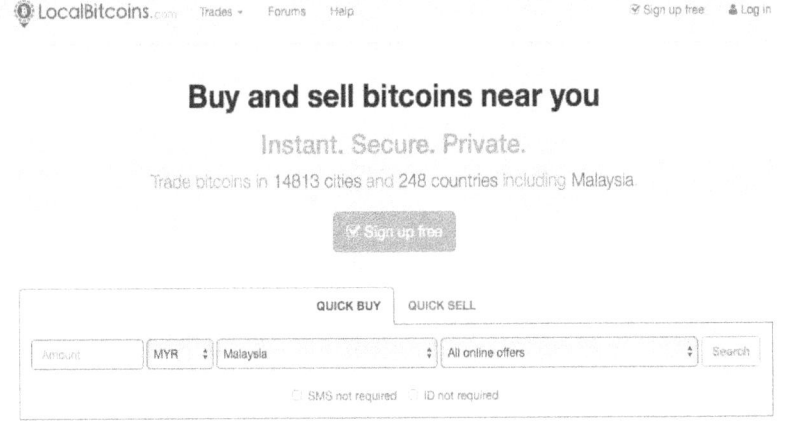

What is a Bitcoin Escrow Agent?

An agent handles the 3rd party escrow service of a Bitcoin transaction. Bitcoin escrow agents are getting more and more common as escrow protects users from fraudulent buyers by requiring the Bitcoin to be deposited upfront. Usually, Bitcoin transactions are anonymous exchanges that involve untrusted parties.

In an event where the sellers turn out to be scammers, the escrow agent will act as an arbitrator and determines who will receive the Bitcoins.

Many Bitcoin marketplace provide escrow services, such as LocalBitcoins, CryptoThrift and BitPremier.

To be an escrow agent, you must build up your reputation as a trustworthy party in the community.

Last but not least is getting involved in Bitcoin affiliate marketing.

For those who are not familiar with affiliate marketing, the idea behind it is that you promote someone else's product and they pay you a percentage of the profit based on the sales you bring in.

Let's illustrate an example. Let's say you decide to promote TREZOR, a hardware cryptocurrency wallet. If a person decides to purchase TREZOR and the customers came from your site, you get a commission for it.

And the best thing is, you earn your commissions in Bitcoin where previous Bitcoin affiliate marketers have reported reasonable values of Bitcoin being paid to them.

I've already listed the possible methods to earn your Bitcoins. Always remember whatever method you choose to venture into, there's no such thing as easy money. If earning Bitcoins were that easy, everyone would have done it by now.

In each of the methods listed above, you will either need to invest your time or your money. There is no easy way out. Try what works for you and be patient with the results.

6. WHY BUY CRYPTOCURRENCY?

Like most things tech, the realm of cryptocurrency can be a bit complex to master and is still new to many. But the advantage of purchasing this currency is surely worth your investment in both time and money. Experts have also predicted that it may be the next big thing in finance.

As a digital asset that serves users online, Cryptocurrency has many appealing benefits.

Some of this is thanks to the Blockchain Technology previously mentioned. It is a strictly monitored process with encrypted transaction and control thus, making this online money a thing for the future.

So in this chapter, we will cover the **top 4 benefits of Cryptocurrency**.

The most well-known benefit of this investment is its '**No Third-Party Involvement**'.

There's always a pattern when using traditional money to buy yourself a new property, setting up your own business, or buying a new car.

One way or another, the process requires a third-party involvement. We are talking lawyers, owners and some others external factors such as, delays, documentations and extra fees. This in general will consume unnecessary time, money and energy to the point of giving up.

A good example of this scenario would be you buying a new house. You need to pay the Financial Advisor who in general, advises your financial statement to ensure you have a stable income.

Some property requires you to pay for a booking fee to 'lock' your house of choice and many other add-ons. In short, there's a lot of third-involvement and it charges you even before you own the property.

But that is not the case with Cryptocurrency. As mentioned previously, the blockchain system is similar to a self-rights database.

It means, the contract is capable of being design and enforces to remove any involvement of the third-party mentioned before. Moreover, the contract can be customized to complete a certain transaction at a set date at a fraction of any expenses.

Yes, you can eliminate any third-party involvement options, in fact, you don't even need one.

In short, you are in control of your own money using Cryptocurrency. This is what we call the 'Decentralized' system, which means there's no 'Central or Federal Government' regulating it for you.

Your transaction is practically immune to any influence from your government and its distinct manipulation.

So, it is possible to be able to pay and receive money anywhere in the world at any given time.

That transaction is done with minimum processing fees, thus preventing users from having to pay extra charges from banks or any financial institutions.

Next advantage would be **the risk it holds is lower than traditional currencies.**

In this era, most people rarely have their cash in their possession now. Instead, they have an array of credit cards, debit cards and other payment cards available as their nations' method of payment.

Nothing's wrong with that, except however if the store's connection to the server is disconnected or their machine is out of service, and you who do not possess any cash just ended up holding the line.

The thing about these cards are, any purchase you are making, you are giving the end-receiver access to your full-credit line. No matter how small the amount of the transaction is, the fact that you are giving someone your card to gain access to your account is already a form of 'breach'.

Most of this 'breach' is considered secure nowadays using differing safety measures like 'PIN enabled' or 'Pay wave' methods.

Then, the store initiates payment by 'pulling' the designated amount from your account using the information provided within your card.

Cryptocurrency doesn't work that way. Instead of a 'pulling' mechanisms, it 'pushes' the amount that needed to be pay or receive to other cryptocurrency holder without any further information needed.

Payments are possible without your personal information being tied to you the transaction. Your account can be backed up and encrypted to ensure the safety of your money.

By allowing users to be in control of their transactions helps keep Bitcoin, Ether or other distinguish Cryptocurrency safe for the network.

Another benefit of using Cryptocurrency would be its **protection from fraud.**

We often heard cases where one's payment card is being used by other users but not the owner. When contacting his card's service issuer, it is found that the card has made certain transactions without his consent. This is what we call a fraud case.

Most of the time these fraud cases get away with the crime because it is not easy to trace the fraud back to the perpetrator. What's more it is even difficult to get the attention of law enforcer to launch an investigation with only a single instance of crime the perpetrator commits.

However, Cryptocurrency is not viable to fraud act. Because your personal information is kept hidden under unnecessary prying eyes, this protects you against identity theft.

Remember, Cryptocurrency is a form of digital money, created from code. Individual cryptocurrencies are as mentioned, digital, and cannot be counterfeited by senders.

Because the transactions cannot be reversed, they do not carry with them any personal information. This ensures security and the merchants are protected from any potential losses that might occur from fraud cases.

It is very hard to cheat or making false pose on anyone using these Cryptocurrencies due to its decentralized system and the existing block chain system. It cannot be manipulated by anyone or organization thanks to it being cryptographically secure.

Lastly would be its **Universality**.

Over the course of payment history, nations worldwide have their differing methods of payments implemented. We have money-goods exchange system and even bartering trade. It is not until traders visited other countries that they found out how to trade items to one another.

Thanks to various innovations and developments, we now have multiple methods to trade and exchange moneys worldwide.

But even with all the upgrades, we are still experiencing problems doing transactions across the globe. There are always currency issues, bank authorizations, unacceptable payment method and some other varying issues experienced by business owners or travelers out there.

Fact is, not all country has similar financial processions. Your card or currency may not be accepted by other countries and that is a major setback to your account.

For example, most online banking, payment or cash system requires additional processing fees for their service even if that account is yours.

However, Cryptocurrencies are not bound by any of those exchange rates, transaction charges, the interest rates or any other fees applied on any countries.

They can be used at any time at any international standard without experiencing any problems.

It also saves a lot of your time and money by reducing additional spending over transferring money from multiple countries to another.

Which means cryptocurrency operates at an international platform which in turns, make transaction easier than your average telegraphic transfer.

To recap, there are 4 major advantages concerning Cryptocurrencies. It has 'No Third-Party Involvement', 'Lower Risk compared to Traditional Currencies', 'Protection from Fraud' and 'Universality'.

Despite the amazing advantages that come with Cryptocurrencies, there are also some setbacks to this investment. We will uncover it in the next chapter.

7. ARE THERE ANY DRAWBACKS ?

Previously, it was mentioned how Cryptocurrency is one of a kind digital currency without likeness. Because not many payments nowadays are without the involvement of a third-party, lower risk payment, little to no fraud cases and most of all, universal in its usage.

However, considering the online nature of Cryptocurrency, there are flaws that come with it. There are 4 major setbacks concerning Cryptocurrency.

The first one is the **lack of understanding over Cryptocurrency**.

In most cases, people are still unaware of the digital currency world and the potential it holds.

This is similar to when the usage of credit card was first announced and the reception towards it is fairly similar to Cryptocurrency. Back then, people wouldn't even think that paying things using a mere card is possible, what's more using a whole new digital currency.

Because it is different, and it doesn't involve cash directly, people shy away from it and constantly doubting its effectiveness. Additionally, it involves online access to make it work.

The idea of having to pay things or transfer money online is convenient to some but most are still skeptical about it.

In order to make Cryptocurrency acceptable around us, the people need to be educated about it to be able to include it in their daily lives.

One way to do it is through networking. But fact is, there are not many places online where people can learn about it.

The effort to learn a whole new world of currency is requires a lot of time and energy. Most would think it is not worth their time because it is not commonly known anyway.

Even though some businesses are accepting bitcoins, the list is significantly small compared to traditional currencies.

This is probably due to the lack of knowledgeable staff that understands the ways of digital currencies. Plus, they need to help educate their customer about it and how to use it for a smooth transaction.

This, again, will take a longer time and effort to teach others.

Another drawback of Cryptocurrency would be its **lack of protection and guarantee**.

In the case of traditional currency, there's Central Bank who governs the authority on every nation's money. No higher authority can suddenly decide that they no longer want to use their country's currency to trade without protest and rejection.

There are proceedings to follow, documents to file, approvals, and many other protocols to follow.

However, that is not the case with our digital currency. There is no Central Bank who governs Bitcoin, which means no one can guarantee its minimum valuation.

The value of Bitcoin for example, will fall tremendously should a major group of merchants decided to just 'discard' Bitcoins and leave the system. This will inevitably put other users who have invest thousands of dollars into Bitcoins into a major loss. There is no one to contact to file these losses, or rules to help compensate it.

Thus, the decentralized system of Bitcoin is what we call a double-edged sword on its own.

The next disadvantage is its **technical shortcomings**.

When online banking made its way to our life, there's always a risk of a sudden server failure, power shortage, and even hardware lags.

If it happens and you ended up getting charge but didn't receive the online movie tickets or flight tickets, you can always call bank service provider, or go to the physical bank instead and declares your case.

Most of the cases if you show evidence of your payment you will get proper compensations or feedbacks.

That is not how it works with Cryptocurrency. First of all, this currency does not have a bank to negotiate and help you around. There is no fixed number that you could call and ask for clarification.

So, if you bought your goods using Bitcoins for example, and the merchant didn't send the items you purchased, there is nothing you can do to reverse the transaction or refund. You can't complain it to the police or any relating authority for that matter.

Similar to data corruptions or virus infections, if you hard drive crashes and your wallet file is corrupted your Bitcoin is lost forever. There is nothing you can you do restore it and those 'coins' will be 'orphaned' in the system.

The last major disadvantage of Cryptocurrency would be because it is **still developing**.

When things are still developing, it is prone to many risks. There are so many incomplete features that can be improved but it takes longer time to finalize it, especially if it has no physical form.

With traditional currency, despite the method of payments nowadays are done online, and without us actually seeing the physical money transferring from one account to another, in the end of the day, when you reach the ATM, you are capable of holding that cash.

You can use it to buy stuff from the stores physically, and online. That shows how developed our traditional currency is.

Since Cryptocurrency does not have any physical forms, its usage is obviously restricted.

It must always be converted to traditional currency to enjoy its worth. According to studies, there was a time when there is a proposition to store Bitcoin wallet information in cards. However, there is neither consensus nor continuation of the proposal.

Most probable reason would be because merchants find it unfeasible to support all the cryptocurrency cards. There is no system for an immediate payment using the cards, thus users are forced to convert it into real money anyway.

As you can see, there are 4 disadvantages of Cryptocurrencies. There is a lack of understanding towards this digital currency. Plus, there's minimum protection and guarantee when using is. Because it is mostly operating online, it is bound to experience all kinds of technical flaws and it is still developing.

The world of cryptocurrency is relatively new to some people and it can be difficult to understand. Because nobody really knows what currencies will or can be adopted and at what scale.

So, in the next chapter we will talk about what the future holds for Cryptocurrency.

8. THE FUTURE OF CRYPTOCURRENCY

Now we will finally touch upon the future of Cryptocurrency.

These digital currencies have been said to be able to capture the world of online finance. With the blockchain technology behind it, the future of Cryptocurrency is showing a prosperous potential.

Starting 2017, the alternative currencies will need to watch its prices closer than usual.

Studies show that Bitcoin experienced a drop in its price. It seems like a cheaper cryptocurrency by the name Ether, reached its highest at $40 a unit. That's right.

Although the mechanism behind Ether prevents it from being used as a direct payment method, this cryptocurrency seems to have brighter future ahead. This is all thanks to its smart contract concepts.

On the other hand, cryptocurrencies who is concerned over privacy are starting to gain more prominent favor amongst users.

Bitcoin, unfortunately despite their security measures, it continues to have loopholes that can be exploited for access to users' personal data. But this doesn't stop users from investing to Bitcoin. Up to this day, Bitcoin is still being accepted as a means of payment.

The level of acceptance is clearly bringing this alternative currency to the mainstream. Some companies are genuinely considering to invest in this currency, further fueling its journey to the world of financial currency.

Are we going to witness a new norm of currency by cryptocurrency one day? Researchers concluded that it is still too early to predict that it would, but one thing is for sure that this currency is slowly making its way to the world.

The most targeted group of all would be the technologically savvy individuals and most of us are already part of this group. More than 50% of our time spent online and it won't be long until it reaches a hundred.

One day, we might even consider using Cryptocurrency as our standard currency for a more universal transaction.

- Thank You -

MESSAGE FROM AUTHOR

Yes, I am special. However, the good news is that I wasn't born that way. I developed it, which means we all have an equal opportunity for success. In fact, I bet you have even more opportunity to succeed than I do, because your parents aren't struggling to feed you. The only person stopping you from success is YOU! Your background doesn't matter. Your country doesn't matter. I strongly believe you will never succeed until you say and live by the saying, "My country will never be an excuse for my failure. My background will never be an excuse for my failure." You should also know that everything starts from the mind. The best way to nurture your great dreams is to keep yourself updated, and surround yourself with positive people.

www.ingramcontent.com/pod-product-compliance
Lightning Source LLC
Chambersburg PA
CBHW050244230526
45470CB00005B/2111